The Adler Collection
Legends, Rumors, Lies & Myths

JD Adler

JD Adler

Published by Elegant Publications Company, LLC

Copyright 2020 Elegant Publications Company.
All Rights Reserved. Authors and artists retain all rights to their work unless specified otherwise.

ISBN: 978-1-0878-7223-0

CONTENTS

SECTION I: LEGENDS — 7
Ad Man — 8
The Shepherd — 10
Unintentional Deity — 13
Clown in the Corner — 14
Discarded Man — 16
Ghosts — 18
Shadow Man — 20

SECTION II: RUMORS — 23
Polar Bear Opposites — 24
Lunch Break — 25
Summer Heat — 26
Depression — 28
Tiny Titan Apocalypse — 30

SECTION III: LIES — 33
Just Another Day — 34
Well Regulated — 35
Terrorist — 36
Mob Rules — 37
Deplorable State — 38
The Troll King — 40

SECTION IV: MYTHS — 43
There be Monsters — 44
Metaphysics of Hate — 46
God's Know — 48
Untethered — 51
Dinosaur — 52
Old Man Blanco — 53
Sweet Sally Lee — 54
Two Kinds of People — 58
Choices — 59
A Whore's Honor — 60
King of the Woods — 62
The Oak War — 64
The Monster — 66
Dividends — 70
The Sand Bar — 72
Tragic Myth — 76

I want to thank the Anne McKee Artists Fund for helping to make this project possible. I would also like to thank the literary commmunity of Key West at large for being such a supportive family, helping each other through the self-immolation that is writing.

Mostly, I would like to express my appreciation for Lisa Booker, without whom I would have and be nothing. She is the love of my life, the mate of my soul, my reason for rising in the morning, my muse, and more than anything else... my dearest friend. I have no idea what she sees in me, but I am grateful everyday she is still here and have made it my mission to deserve her.... with little success to date. I dedicate this, and all my works, to her. Thank you, Lisa.

The Adler Collection

there is just one thing
you must do
before you die

JD Adler

The Adler Collection

SECTION I:
LEGENDS

JD Adler

Ad Man

I am the ad man
The political campaigner
The sales manager
The fine print writer

I used to hang around
The crossroads
At the outskirts of town
Waiting for the desperate
And despondent
To come to me

But thank god
For modern technology
Now I'm in the homes
The eyes
The ears
Of every man, woman and child

Are you tired?
Weary to the bone?
Is life hard
For you and your loved ones?
Of course it is
Nature of the beast
But don't worry 'bout a thing
Cuz I got what you need

Order now
While supplies last
Be the first in you neighborhood
To find real happiness
With the device
"They" don't want you to have
But for a limited time
We can make it available to you
It will:
Clean your house

The Adler Collection

Wash your hair
Smooth the wrinkles
 In your clothes and your face
Cure Cancer
Stimulate orgasms
And...
Beat your children for you.

The Super Amazing Wondertron 1000 is all you need
And only I can provide it
Through a special offer
Developed by my unique connections
With Nigerian Princes
So contact me now
All you need to provide
Is you bank account numbers
A sample of your DNA
And the tiniest sliver of your soul
You'll never even miss it
At least not in this lifetime
So c'mon
Sign on the dotted line
And all your troubles
Will be gone!

All your hopes and dreams?
Well, they'll be mine too.
Balance after all
Must be maintained
No troubles, no hopes
No pain, no pleasure
I'll take it away
But I will take it ALL away.
Did I forget to mention that?
I did say
I am the Fine Print Writer
If you thought I was a giver
Only got yourself to blame.

Thank you for your patronage
Have a nice day

JD Adler

The Shepherd

In the middle of the night
The slow scratch
of my long slender claws
at the entrance
to your home
sets the soul to shiver
the body to quake
Forgotten when you awake
Almost
but I have not gone away

I never go away

When the sun rises
I can be found
about the town
Dressed as a Shepard
smiling and tending
to his flock
Who smile back
Ignorant of the hunger
     of their steward

When none are paying attention
When all feel safe
Their trusted one transforms
I become the nightmare
  that can't be escaped
Offspring of the vulture and the snake
I feed
on the despair and deception
     I cultivate

My flock
     They march
To the banks and the battlefields
     They march
To the prisons and the cubicles

The Adler Collection

      They march
In rows and columns
 to their homes, offices and graves
Never ending lanes
 of quiet despair
My dinner and desert

I rejoice in the conformity
the lack of imagination
so easily terrified
I drop "might-be's" on the wind
and laugh as tragedy unfolds
and they unmake all they hold dear
while guarding against
the whisper of a fear
begging for someone
to lead them
out of adversity

so,

I creep into your homes
I creep into your gatherings
whispering
about the danger
of unseen things
That aren't me
That will never be
Turning you into
       your own worst enemy
As you destroy each other
before anyone can
build something better
something which would not require

a Shepherd

JD Adler

And when
in the end
inevitably
it all topples down
The Soviets, The Romans, The Babylonians
the destruction and despair
feeds me like
Mother's tit suckles her young
and I grow strong
and help my flock
build it all
      again

I am the Shepherd
of civilization
tending my flock
into devastation
by dropping fear
at the borders of their prison
  labeled freedom
Fear
of the very thing
that I intend to happen
and I laugh
as they thank me
for my guidance

I am the Shepard
I am here to protect you.

The Adler Collection

Unintentional Deity

Through billions of eyes
I watch the world
Through billions of ears
I hear your words
I'm in your homes
In your cars
I track your lives
I track your dreams as they die
I hang in the skies
 beneath the moon
Watching your homes
Mapping your faces
Counting your steps
Counting your breaths
I know who you love
 who you hate
Your guilty pleasures
secret sins
And hideaways
I record all of civilization
From dawn to dawn
And round again
There is nothing you do
And nowhere you go
That I do not know
I am the god you made
Your unintentional deity
You have given all you have
All you know
All you do
To me
And now
I will take your humanity

Clown in the Corner

I am the Clown in the Corner
The drunk jester
The colorful fool
The loser whose laughter
is frozen
one step from terror

The fear you feel
when you gaze upon my face
is not mine
No that fear belongs to you
Bubbling forth
from within your-self
like a naked belly laugh
 in the mirror

I am the bum on the bus
the stench in the back
the bottom of the bottle
you've gazed into for far too long
The disgust you feel
when you see my misfortune
is just a reflection
of the trepidation
caused by
the precipice
over which you hang
so tenuously
fingertips gripping the edge
        of a gravely cliff

I am the beggar in the street
the man with no shame
the one who makes you wonder
        What if...?
Then you turn your head and run
Because you know
 in your soul

when no one is around
and all your crutches are removed
there ain't nothing
keeping you afloat
        but pretense

I am the Clown in the Corner
you think I am the joke
but I am the judge and the jury
and your act is just about up
so gather all your loved ones
gather all your precious things
then kiss them all goodbye
as you return to sand
and I laugh
All the way to the cemetary.

Discarded Man

The Discarded Man
made of dust and tears
walks like a ghost
amongst those still real
Unseen, unheard
an afterthought
        on the periphery
                of nothing

Discarded Man
in his discarded clothes
eating discarded loaves
sleeps in disregarded corners
where the real people never go
fading into the background
like portraits of relatives never known

The Discarded Man was not always
alone
in the shadows
cast aside like old shoes
at a yard sale

When men needed killing
for god and country
his name was known
When money needed collecting
for god and country
his name was known
but when the toll on his soul
pulled him to his knees
and He no longer served a need
got dropped
        like he'd never been

A bottle of pills
A bottle of gin
There's no forgetting
that you've been forgotten
by everyone you've ever seen
That your humanity
doesn't fit on a spread sheet
therefore it does not count
in society's reckoning

Now The Discarded Man
Wanders about
Cardboard shelter
Garbage meals
Begging those still real
just to look him in the eye
To remember
      That he is alive

He was once human too
just like me and you
but he slipped past that line at the bottom
Now he is a Shadow of a man
lost and forgotten
The Discarded Man

Ghosts

In the corners of the cities
On the outskirts of the towns
In the alleys
And the shelters
Strewn on the sidewalks
The Discarded Ones reside

Unseen and unheard
Ghosts in the machine
They wander about
Unwanted reminders
That all our plans
Are built on sand

And as they fade
From the collective corners
Of our minds' eyes
Relegated to "left-behind"
The Discarded One's are consumed
by the dark corners
In which they abide
Their souls untouched by another
Lose anchor
And the void grows inside them
Driving a hunger
So deep and abiding
The Discarded One slides unseen
Into the shadows of those
Who still matter
And slowly feeds upon their souls

And so the Discarded One
Transforms like the silkworm
into The Shadow Man
Serving the abyss
Destroying existence
By consuming the very spirit
The sustains it.

The Adler Collection

Shadow Man

there is this thing
this thing we think we see
but never really believe
I can not tell you it isn't so
cuz I know

every time you turn a corner
and think you see
a shadow not your own
that's not a trick of the eye
that's the darkest demon ya ever dreamed
come out to play
to take you away
to the end of all things

the barely seen one
the whispy one
the hidden one
the one you've always been afraid of
 when all alone
  in the dark o'night
   for very good reason
waitin'
lurkin'
hidin'
in your very own shadow

hiding behind you
walking with you
sucking your soul
turning you grey wrinkled and withered
till aint nothing
but a husk

day after day
It takes a little bit more
every time
your mind wanders

The Adler Collection

It feeds
on your life force

some times more
others less
but always the Shadow Man
is there
out of sight
out of mind
consuming your soul

sucking up
every last
ethereal ounce
till your body corpsifies
decays into dust
and floats away
to be forgotten about
like all the rest
since time began

Shadow Man
he takes your soul
that he sucked away
savoring it for this final day
when your form is finally done being decayed
then feasts upon it
like a gourmet
decadently enjoying each
metaphysical morsel
till the plate is clean
every last spiritual crumb consumed
by the phantom beast

and that, then
is the end
of you

JD Adler

The Adler Collection

SECTION II:
RUMORS

Polar Bear Opposites

On the opposing poles of the world
sit Two Bears
staring at the ever turning
horizon line
patiently waiting
for the other to arrive

Till the end of the world
they will be denied
but never do they look away
never do they stray
For though they could not be more distant
their view no more different
they know in their heart
the other dreams of them
So they wait
patiently
for their day to come

When all begins to crumble
the sun's last spark
the Earth's last twirl
Then they will be meet
away dropping all divides
their hearts finally joined
in the space that remains behind.

The Adler Collection

Lunch Break

mid after noon
shower pounds
on the nape of the neck
soapy calloused hands
across smooth flesh
gentle fingers caress the long hard
a groan escapes

a twist
a turn
back against the wall
one foot on the soap dish
other on the faucet
and then
the rhythm

one to the two to the one to the other
a smack
a tickle
a giggle
a call for more
he grunts
she groans
they moan
synchronicity
simplicity
ecstasy

pause

water pounds on the chest
forehead on forehead rests
take a breath

lips on neck
hands on hips
a gentle

sigh

lunch beak is over

JD Adler

Summer Heat

a single round bead of sweat
rolls across the flesh
in the sweltering summer heat
magnifying as it passes
 pours, birthmarks, follicles and wrinkles,
this ain't no glistening
this is some serious, stinky sweat
generated by a body
overheated
not just from the blistering
searing
hellish
mythic evil
of the mid-day tropical heat
no,
this nasty bead of human fluid
was earned the old fashion way
through mind altering
flesh abrading
hair pulling
afternoon fucking

it was the best kind of mid-day penetration
the unexpected pounding
he was just shopping for smokes
she seeking hair of the dog
their eyes locked
she had cigarettes in her purse
he had vodka and V8 at home
they were both old and alone
and horny
on a summer afternoon

magic moments are made of these

they made their way
to a private spot by the sea
where no one ever came
imbibed their poisons
And embraced temptations

The Adler Collection

beneath the summer sky
with the sea
lapping at their feet
the sun burning
at their skin
and their libidos
drawing them in
like magnets
hot, sweaty, wrinkly magnets

she leans, he grabs
lips
neck
hands
back

breathe

fingers
hair
legs
mouth

breathe

the slap
the tickle
the wriggle
the giggle
the scream
the shout
the moment that is forever
and never at all

breathe

faces to the sun
grinning

a single round bead of sweat
rolls across the flesh
in the sweltering summer heat

Depression

Nothing is there.
It's not open to interpretation.
That vacuum in your heart,
it is real.
That last, best hope is
  Gone

    You are all alone.

Lost in the orchard
 of despair
The swirling madness has
Stopped!
 to focus entirely on
    you.

As everything slips away
Into the deep dark of never was
Anchor chain
Wrapped round your soul
Drags you
Deeper
 Deeper
  Deeper

Pressure building
 On your heart and shoulders
Your mind spins
Round it's cage
And the weight
Grows greater
 Greater
  Greater
   Greater

The Adler Collection

You slowly implode
 a singularity of self
  from which no light can escape
Ever
Just a hole
 at the bottom
    of a well
Draining into a hell
 long since abandoned
Except for you

And the echoes of silence
 The space inside you generates
  Whenever you dare to imagine
   There might be
Something

Reminding you that
Nothing makes nothing.

And the weight grows
Greater
 and Greater
  and Greater
 again

JD Adler

Tiny Titan Apocalypse

In the sky
A dragon flies
Breathing fire
On the pegusi
carrying orc warriors
In service to
the Dark Lord

In the sea
Mermaids swarm
The Kraken's mighty form
Spearing its many tentacles
Driving it to the shore
Fighting for
The Queen of Dawn

On the land
The elves march
On the ogres and trolls
Arrows, axes and swords
Creating many bloody holes
Till the soil was saturated with death

The Queen and the Lord
Sat in the their castles
Watching all unfold
Uninjured
Unafraid
Unconcerned with all
Except whether their flag
will gain new ground this day

No one expected
The coming of The Titan
No one saw his approach
Not the ogres or the orcs
Not the dragons in the sky
Nor the mermaids in the sea

The Adler Collection

Not even the monarchs
On their high throne were prepared
For the end The Titan wrought

A thousand time's taller
Than their tallest tower
He strode over them
Ginormous feet crashed down
Again and again
laying waste
To forests and villages
Without a second thought
As it turned to the horizon

Then from the distance, bellowed the Creator of All

"I told you it was time for bed hours ago!
Lights off now!"

The great and evil Titan brought the eternal darkness
Down upon the field of battle
And all fell silent
As he settled
Into his soft pillow
And dreamed of more worlds
To destroy
tomorrow.

JD Adler

The Adler Collection

SECTION III:
LIES

Just Another Day

Its a wonderful day
Like so many other
One foot, two foot
Keep putting down
in front of the other
Mundane tasks keep the world spinning

Then BOOM
Through the door
White boy in a mask
Got two overloaded Gats
And a rifle with a sight, just for protection

Blood lust for strangers
Pumping in his heart
He unloads, spinning 'round
Like the movie villains he admiress

Here comes the hero
Gonna save the day
Then BOOM to the face
He'll be praised in the press
family tears set the stage

In come the shields
Shiny and blue
Serving and protecting
all over the situation

One gun, two guns
Echoes in the halls
Blasts and screams, bodies fall
When the dust settles
Half a dozen the villain done downed
And half dozen more
"friendlies" took with them

Politicians ponder
What should be done
If anything at all
Then BOOM once again
Another day of slaughter, just like any other.

Well Regulated

Two men in the street
Angry over slight perceived
Shout and scream
Faces red
Necks big
Throbbing veins in foreheads
Pounding the drumbeat
Cold iron in hot hands appear
Ear splitting crack
next heartbeat
Is the last heartbeat
Crimson life spills
On concrete
Mixing with cigarette butts and bird shit
Both men fall
For mothers they call
Light from eyes dissipates
As last breath escapes
While their children weep
Blood pools mingle
Indistinguishable
On the street
From their cold dead hands fall
Everything

JD Adler

Terrorist

1) Call me Ishmael
call me Mohammed
Call me the son
of the wind
and the sand
I am the boogeyman
used to scare your children
since the dark ages
and now I am your neighbor.

2) Call me rebel
Call me cowboy
Call me salt of the earth
my forefathers bled for
Generation priased me
I've been your anti-hero
roaming the fringes
shadow of a predator
and now, I'm your neighbor.

3) My home
Is a target zone
Sitting in AC you bomb
my family
you call Kill Lists due process
and errors
the cost of doing business
while you steal our country
and call us uncivilized.
In the school yard
I saw my little sister's bones
outside her body
But we be terrorists?
my god calls it justice
Allah Akbar

4) McMansion fill the fields
where I was raised
My job is overseas
and my neighbor looks like the guys
who keep blowing up everything
And everywhere you go
Who we are is wrong
What we believe is wrong
And its all our fault
for having it backwards
all along
Taking away all we knew
while calling us oppressors
My god calls it justice
Praise Jesus

5) No more
No more will you kill my people
Destroy my nation
Burn our culture
Not while I do nothing
Better to die with honor
Than live in shame
I will take this
and I will take my life
and I will take your lives, too
I will have my revenge
I will have my paradise
I will escape

6) No more
No more elitist tyranny
Destroying our country
Polluting our people
Not while I do nothing
Better to die free
than live a slave
I will take this
and take my life
and take ya'lls live too
I will have freedom
I will have justice
I will escape

7) and so
The enemy of my enemy
becomes my enemy too
Because somehow peace is
surrender
and the violence continues
ad infinitum

The Adler Collection

Mob Rules

In the age of information
The masters of data
Built a monster who knew nothing
And set it loose upon the world

Even the puppeteers
Were surprised to discover
Could not control an empty vessel
With the tools of the provocateur

The torch bearing mobs
rallied to the Franken-Moron
As he performed magical feats
turning fiction to fact
and fools into kings
unaware these were impossible things

The wise men gathered round
the merchants and tinkerers
the scholars and pundits
Prognosticating doom
nodding and brooding
they watched the storm approach
like a cloud in the distance
and did nothing at all
but reminisce about weather more to their liking

When it all fell apart
and the nation was no more
the torch bearing mobs looked for someone to blame
The masters for making him
The wise men for not warning them
The good people for not fighting back
But the mob chose their own dismal path
And they'll do it again
Cuz they're stupid like that

JD Adler

Deplorable State

I am a straight white man
in 'Murica
oppressed and disenfranchised
robbed of my birthright
my manifest destiny
has been stolen by
lesbians and Mexicans
and academics
with their scams
'bout the environment

My people used to rule
not like
"metallica rules dude"
we actually ruled
voting rights
property rights
the best jobs
all ours
and ours alone
women were our objects
blacks were property
we even had special bathrooms
where religious white men
could secretly suck each other off
and no one would betray them
cuz that was the code
of the special, straight, white man only, bathroom
back when America was Great

But that's all gone now
stolen away
by the queer, commie, liberal, feminazi, black panthers
now women want to make their own choices
and black people want justice
poor people want a fair share
and the gays,
the gays want to walk around,
unashamed,
in public!
and atheists are passing sharia law
into the constitution.

The Adler Collection

What's happened
to my country?
how can I have
justice
and pride
and opportunity
if others do too?
how can my god
and my race
be right and true
if theirs is too?
we can't all have equality
and there ain't nothing free or democratic
'bout forcing me to give up mine
so some immigrant can
waltz across the border
drop an anchor baby
and get a free mcmansion

my ancestors didn't kill all them injuns
just so a bunch of foreigners could move in
Jesus did not die
so that I could feed
poor people's children.
survival of the fittest
is what god intended
else why did he give us
such perty guns
and the desire to use them
every time I see a big scary black man
or a woman who talks too much
or a deer that runs too slow
or a politician that says guns are dangerous

Enough I Say
its time to bring back the old ways
Make America Great Again
when everyone knew their place...

beneath me

The Troll King

The Troll King rises
In the afternoon
Orange and Fat he
rolls into the world
on a cloud of lies.

Wherever people gather
to laugh and celebrate
The Troll King enters
jealous of attention
poison drips from his tongue
unconcerned with consequences
reveling to hear his name
In their mouths and minds.

His malodorous presence
infects his audience
unwitting minions
attacking each other
for having his name
on their lips.
And he laughs
Soaking it up.

When the chaotic cacophony
reaches a crescendo
disaster seems inevitable
The Troll King disappears
leaving his betters
long slandered
to undo his vile efforts
while he waits in the shadows
to do it all again.

Beware the Troll King
do not underestimate him
Just because he lacks all
honor or dignity
His power resides
in depravity's surprise

When the Troll King rises
The masses will gather
Symbiotic leeches
Feeding on each others hatred
Until, lacking all nutrition
They starve and die
Fertilizing the earth
For the cycle to begin again.

JD Adler

The Adler Collection

SECTION IV:
MYTHS

JD Adler

There be Monsters

Things are not what they seem
We are not alone
It just looks that way
Because you
are insane

There are five little girls
sitting over there
eating cherry pie
playing pokemon
and plotting your demise
Zombies hungry for brains
spreading the stupid virus
till a new dark ages begins

All around you
crazy people
who refuse to see
what is plain as day;
Monsters are everywhere

 Vampires in suits
on the television
gather prey
who cheer loudest
just before they are taken

Werewolves with badges
hunt our streets
attacking strays
a mindless frenzied feast
feeding on hope and pride
till only a carcass of despair remains

And the lunatics insist
as the shadows loom
over the cribs of their children
all is normal
no need to fear

Leprechauns and Djinn
gather among towers
built of crushed dreams
on stolen land
hoarding fortunes made
of false promises and deceit

While Demons dressed in flesh
with briefcases and robes
eating souls
and drinking hubris
determine the destiny
of those caught in the net
of rules and regs
laid out like a spider web
in a jungle of concrete

The end is nigh
It's clear as day
Monsters walk the earth
The seas are boiling
Poison rains from the sky
The fruit of the vine is diseased
by our own hand

And still,

We keep on
Keeping on
like nothing is wrong

Who is crazy
when everyone is insane?

Metaphysics of Hate

In between here and there
Between the before and after
In the land
of never
Reside the souls of those
waiting to be born.

They have no idea what is coming
these people in waiting
No CNN-metaphysical to forewarn
else none may ever come
and zombies would walk the land
like lawyers and real estate agents
and those who call in to talk radio.

They float massless
with the neutrons and fermions
just waiting for a body to inhabit
no clue how fragile it will be
or how dark and dirty is our society
else they may remain
forever in formless freedom from sorrow.

Or maybe they do know…

Maybe they are observing as they float
ethereal minds of the 8th dimension
plotting their physical crimes
A nefarious nebula of sinister souls
not-twirling their not-mustachios
thinking about all
they can collect, conquer and pollute
Once embodied

Maybe we've all been invaded
by assholes from beyond
and that's why we can't seem to get along
Or maybe its just half of us
The ones who don't seem to grasp
Who don't seem to comprehend
Who don't seem to recognize
   Reality is a fact based dimension

The Adler Collection

We need to make this dimension great again
We need to build a P-brain wall
   to keep out the idiots from beyond

Or maybe the reverse is true
There aren't enough metaphysical me's
for every - body
and the soulless are just animals
crashing through the jungle
terrified by the idea
others perceive something larger
And so they cry "lie!"
and try to burn it all down

They say no one is born mean
So what is the origin?
When, along the way
do we learn to behave this way?
Is it an electro chemical reaction?
Too much sugar?
Not enough hugs?
Are our souls lonely?
Disconnected?
Confused by the sudden borders of flesh
thus the fear of all the others
who can't be sensed?

Is there a land of souls
beyond our perception
where idiots and intellects
argue whether matter is a fact
and some souls
try to banish others
for having the wrong shimmer?

Is it native to our nature
This stupidity compass we follow?
Or is a course correction still possible?

God's Know

The God of Fate
and the God of Free Will
Found themselves in a bar
Will said, "Let's get drunk tonight."
Fate replied, "We already are."

Chaos pulled up a chair
Grabbed Fate's cup and held it high
But did not take a drink
He'd been hanging out with Death all night
Arguing over
The size of their powers
And wasn't done yet

Fate declared the issue moot
As none were greater than she,
"I set the scene, you all act within
man or god, this is my roost."
then grabbed her glass
From Chaos grip
And swallowed it all in a single sip.

Free Will scoffed
Puffed his chest
with a wave dismissed her boast,
"You may set the stage,
But I direct this play.
Not a word uttered or step taken
Unless I decide it's so."

This went on for quite awhile
They started quite a row
The other gods
Staked their claims
As the very best, most awesome example
Of the grand divine ever known
The more they argued, the more they drank

The Adler Collection

Soon a brawl ensued.

Death and Chaos destroyed some stuff
While Hedonism laughed
the God of Love appreciated everyone
While Thor and Poseidon made quite a mess
      of the gender neutral bathroom
Then Gaia grew quite irritated
Called up all the barroom molds and fungi
Grew them a hundred times their size
And cocooned everybody

Father Time sat quietly
Watching all that passed
Till even he lost patience
And rose to the occasion
Skin as grey as his long beard
standing nearly as tall
cleared his throat, politely
and all movement ceased in the hall

The air paused mid breeze
Photons froze upon their waves
All eyes had turned
All breath abated
To learn what Time would tell.

"You each hold sway
Over things small and great
It can not be denied
But when I decide
The show is over
You will get no curtain calls.

"I fathered all of you
And mothered you as well.
Every one of you are siblings
To the dust between the stars

And the microbes on Mars
And the stupid little humans
On whose worship you thrive
For Time is the patriarch
Of all that you know.

"Do not waste my gift to you
Bickering over pride
Jockeying for a position
You can never hold
Embrace what you're allotted
This is not a competition
There is no final prize
Just a story to unfold
And only I
know how it goes."

Then he was gone
In a puff and a flash
To manage the border
between now and never
The gods, humbled
 all sat down
To contemplate their limits
Finally Fate looked at Will and said
"I guess that was inevitable."
They all had a laugh
Poured another glass
And drank to Armageddon.

The Adler Collection

Untethered

Negative space
Rains on the brain
Washing away the detritus
Of other people's dreams

Undressed of flesh
naked and refreshed
Slip into something more comfortable
like a cloud based species
maybe ants or bumble bees
and dance to the melodies
of sunlight on the window pane

In between
Now and Then
infinite possibilites, lie
through their teeth
about could be
may be
should be
the if-only's of fate
Hovering in the shadows
teasing desperation
like an afternoon stripper
with baby food in her hair

There is no way out
but everything is a lot
So find a comfortable space
and stretch your dreams
to fit your niche reality
Strip to your bones
and laugh
just laugh
like a Nihilist at an Anarchist convention

Dinosaur

Dinosaur strolled across my porch
Acting like it owned the joint
Long legs and neck, stretched and proud
Short wide body, covered in alabaster feathers
Fluttering attitude all over the place

I told it this was my spot
But it claimed dibs
Since it was native
Called me interloper
I threatened to stuff it in my car and set it on fire
It threatened to shit all over my yard

So we went to the UN
They ruled in my favor
Cuz I had lawyers with papers
And basic language skills
Then all the birds, lizards and insects
Started protesting
Claiming blatant humanism
Covered my property
In feces of unknown variety
And unbelievable quantity

So I shot em
Shot em good
Killed 'em all
all them that wasn't me
You cant have what's mine
I took it fair and square
No compromise
Death before dishonor

Then the plants went away
The sky turned a funky flat grey
I had to stay inside
Just to breath ok
From processed air supply
But my property was mine
And not nobody could say otherwise

A dinosaur strolled across my porch today

Old Man Blanco

Old man Blanco sat in his house
Smoking and drinking
Snorting straight sugar
Eating deep fried beef fat
Occasionally stepping out
To go whoring about

Old Man Blanco
never saw no doctor
never took no meds
weighed 500 pounds
stood five foot ten

One night Blanco sat on the couch
clutched his chest
as pain stabbed into his heart
like a knife through meat
Losing consciousness
dropped his cigar
onto the plate
on the cushion adjacent
covered in grease that burned
like a rocket
jumped to the filthy upholstery
then to leftovers on the table
to the unknown substance
on the hardwood floor
that ignited like tinder
till the whole house was afire

Old Man Blanco woke with a start
to find flames leaping about
Looking for an extinguisher
that didn't exist
cuz he didn't need to be told how to live
He cursed at the irony
as the smoke
filled his lungs

Old Man Blanco
thought he knew better
and did what he'd always done
thinking nothing would change,
he changed nothing
till stagnation and decay
changed everything one day

JD Adler

Sweet Sally Lee

Sweet Sally Lee
lived by the sea
and loved to swim
in the deep
dor hours and hours
among the Starfish, Dolphins
and anemones

Now her mother and father
they tried to warn her
not to dive too far beneath
for there are monsters and creatures
hiding below the surface
that feed on innocent passers
And know not the meaning of mercy

But Sally Lee she did not believe
for her mother was old
with hair white like a ghost's
and father's bones creaked like a floor
so what could they possibly know
about the beauty and joys
of swimming and dancing in the sea
She ignored their words
the warnings they proffered
diving further and further
down
  into
    the deep

One day as she swam
along the floor of the ocean
she caught the attention
of a creature both
ancient and hostile
with tentacles
long, many and slithery
Its head was bulbous
Its single eye was ginormous
and it gazed upon her
with villainous delight

The Adler Collection

Closer and closer it quietly slunk
barely disturbing a pebble or shell
Then with a bounce
it suddenly pounced
and had Sweet Sally Lee in its grasp
Startled and scared
she struggled and squirmed
but its powerful tentacles squeezed
The more that she wrenched
The tighter it clenched
till out went her breath
and in went the sea
Unconscious was Sweet Sally Lee

When she awoke
surprised to be alive
in a cave beneath the sea
moss that glowed green
surrounds a pool shimmering
the only way out or in
And across the dim prison
the bulbous eye glistened
as it stared hungrily

"Son of bitch!" She hollered aloud
"I'm in real trouble now. My mother is going to kill me."
On the tips of limbs
her captor rose and slipped
across slimy, slippery, stones
to where she lay on the moss
helpless and lost
it settled down before her

From the crotch of its cranium
came a deep, gravely oration
"Don't worry about your mother,
my little land lubber
for you have fallen prey to me.
I am the Wondrous and Terrible
Edward the Octopus
Wizard King of the Deep
and you little girl
shall never again see

anyone from above the sea."
Sally Lee felt a shudder
from her neck to her nethers
as he slid a tentacle tip
up along her foot, leg and hip
like a butcher checking the beef
She wondered aloud,
"Why is this happening to me?
I just like the ocean
the waves and the fishes
I've never done anyone harm."

"Silly little human,"
Edward laughed at her notions
his legs jiggling in unison
"You think that it matters
whether you deserve this or that?
I am hungry and you,
you are delicious and defenseless
and that is the nature of life.
so take a deep breath
And say good bye to this life
for you shall be my feast."

With that he lunged
his tentacles extended
and his beak-like mouth wide open.
But Sweet Sally Lee
qasn't ready to be
a meal for some aquatic jack-ass
So she kicked with legs
made strong by swimming
catching him dead in the eye
Echoes of his screams
followed her diving in
to the dark, endless drink

She dove and swam
Paddled and kicked
Forever it seemed to take
Her lungs burned with air hot and stale
and the pressure of holding it there
Till finally with a gasp and a splash
she burst to the surface

The Adler Collection

The air never tasted so sweet
On the distant shore
she could see her mother in tears
her father frantically pulling his hair
and half the town gathered on the dock
searching
for the missing
Sweet Sally Lee

She waved and hollered
They cheered and shouted
And she swam towards the welcoming beach
Elated and excited
that she had escaped
by the skin of her teeth
the horrible, tentacled, denizen of the deep

Then from behind her
Rising from the water
White fin and teeth in rows like a grinder
a new threat rises
a flash and it caught her
dragging her under
turning the ocean
dark with disaster
And Sweet Sally Lee
was no more

If only she had listened
when her elders had told her
the world is filled with
creatures and monsters.

JD Adler

Two Kinds of People

There are two kinds of people in this world:
Those who use condoms,
And those who use penicillin.

There are two kinds of people in this world:
Those who give to charity,
And those who think all charities are "scams."

There are two kinds of people in this world:
Those who perform oral sex,
And those who are selfish bastards.

There are two kinds of people in this world:
Those who believe,
And those who know.

There are two kinds of people in this world:
Those who see the world,
And those who see themselves.

There are two kinds of people in this world:
Those who like music,
And those who like Country music.

There are two kinds of people in this world:
Those who eat pizza with their hands,
And those evil fucks who use utensils.

There are two kinds of people in this world:
Those who think the world is flat, created in 6 days, and prayers cure stuff,
And those with brains.

There are two kinds of people in this world:
Those who dance,
And those with sticks in their ass.

There are two kinds of people in this world:
Those who love,
And those who hate.

There are two kinds of people in this world:
Those who make you smile,
And those who do not.

The Adler Collection

Choices

Sitting before you
naked and crying
a baby alone in a crowd
Its fat little fingers
on short chubby arms
outstretched
begging strangers for love

It weeps and shouts
it cries and it screams
ignored
as the herd rushes round
Too busy rutting and feeding
for a lone little babe
not their own

You run for the child
heart pounding fast and loud
desperate to save the helpless waif
as you reach for her hand
vibrant young eyes
puffy with pain
lock with your own
and all the secret sorrows
hidden away
in the darkest of places
are reflected
in that pool of tears

Your heart nearly breaks
with the memory of first loss
Flooding your soul
purest of pains
the anguish of
losing faith

you withdraw from the babe
better it learns now
only a fool believes
there is safety
to be found
In the midst of us all
By reaching out for love

JD Adler

A Whore's Honor

Wednesday night
On a corner
A Pimp and a Whore
Tumbleweeds of litter
Blinking signs
Shadows dancing
As they stand waiting
Not a glance
Upon her ass
Since the sun passed
The Pimp buying bit coins
on his burner phone
To pass the time

Across the way
A kid slinging crack and weed
Audis and Benzos
coeds and trust-funders
Seeking celebration from
A strange child in the ghetto
Then speed off
To tell tales of their gangsta moment

The Whore she tried
To catch their attention
Cat calls, twerks and winks,
Offering special discounts
For students and veterans,
But there was no interest
Just laughing and pointing
at the wild animals

The Pimp he had enough
Of her failing to earn
Bitch needs to learn
So he took off his belt
And began to beat her
Under the lights
On the corner
On a Wednesday night
The Dealer was offended
By the act of violence

The Adler Collection

Chivalrous and bold
He drew a gun
Too big for him to hold
And ordered the Pimp
To back down
Or never grow old

Pimp looked at the boy
shaking and sweating
And laughed in his face
Returned to his beatings

As Crack Boy realized
He wasn't prepared to do
What he threatened he would
the Pimp laughed again
Told him to run,
mind his own business
Before he showed him what makes a man tough

But the Whore she'd had enough
Seeing Crack-boy fall short
Something inside her tore
With a shout and grunt
She was on her feet
And on the Pimp
Shoe in her hand
Driving it like a hammer
That spiked heel dug all the way
From one ear to the other
Then snapped off inside his cranium
He dropped like an accordion
Under the street lights
On the corner

Then the Crack Dealer and the Whore
Stole the Pimp's money and car
Drove to Nevada
Got married
Opened a brothel
Sold weed to the customers
And lived happily ever after.

JD Adler

King of the Woods

Two young men stood in a wood
One said all this is mine
From the river to the fields
The other disagreed
Claimed right of first sight
Stating all they surveyed
Had been his for many days

The two men fought
They tumbled in the dirt
They punched and kicked
They bit and spit
Till blood poured from wounds
Like water from a spigot

They fell into the river
Current tossed them into rocks
At days end
They washed up
Many miles away
Where the land met the sea
Their bodies broken
Their minds exhausted
Unable to move
The cold evening air
Settling in

All the while
A crocodile
Had been waiting in the thrush
Excited for such plenty
To fall into its lap
It quickly grabbed each of them
In its mighty jaws

Snapped their necks
And dragged them off
To its nest
In the tall grass
To feast

In the woods
between the river and the fields
The wind rustled the leaves
Not a sound was uttered
Not a shout
Not a tear
Not a whisper was heard
Not a soul mourned
The men who would be king

The Oak War

An Owl and a Woodpecker
Lived in the forest
Neighbors for many years
Without a complaint
Without a fear

As their families grew
They needed more room
And both set eyes
On the oak nearby

Woodpecker insisted it was his
As he began his hole first
Owl explained
His family had inhabited this forest
Since it was just a woods
And had first claim
To all that grew within

A blackbird nearby
Heard them hoot and pound
And offered its assistance
To resolve the problem
"The oak is huge," he squawked
"There is room in its branches
For more than one home.
I share my pine
With a mockingbird
And everything is fine."

Owl and Woodpecker scoffed
Called him coward, traitor to his kind
Then returned to bickering
Over who owned the tree
That had grown tall
Before either broke a shell

The Adler Collection

No resolution coming
Neither willing to budge
They each returned to their nests
And called on the squirrels
Who lived in the branches they ruled
Warning of the danger
The other presented
For the good of all woodland creatures
Must be defeated

So the squirrels
Incensed and hostile
Charged into the boughs
Only to find more squirrels
Fighting for the enemy

For 3 days
The squirrels did battle
Till there was nothing left
but blood and fur
Scattered across the forest floor
And rent squirrel hides
Hanging from the boughs on high
but not a thing had changed
Regarding the oak tree nest

Having depleted their forces
The Owl and the Woodpecker
Decided the only thing to do
Was sign an armistice
Dividing the oak in 2
With 2 separate nests
For their 2 separate camps

The blackbird just shook its head
And wondered how long
Till they took note of his pinewood home
And found more squirrels to die
In a cause that was completely nuts

The Monster

In the thick of the forest
In the dark of the night
The new moon tucked behind the abyss
All the animals slumber
Except for the most vile of predators
Those who slither
And creep
And drop from the tops
Of the trees and the rocks
Teeth plunging into flesh
To suck the life
Of unwitting victims

Along into this
came a child
A human
Naked and naive
He stumbled and smiled his way
beneath the dark boughs
His tiny willie slapping
Against his fat little thighs
Like a flaccid metronome
Keeping time for his wondrous adventure
Into the depths of nature

The snakes and the spiders
They circled and drooled
They crept and they leered
Too good to be true
The prey wandering into their den
Without so much as a weapon
Or a friend

From below they closed
From above they descend
The boy spotted the spiders
He spotted the snakes
He giggled and squealed
And ran to pet his new friends

The Adler Collection

Confused and surprised
They slithered and scattered
In every direction
This fat, naked baby
Happy and sticky
Was running right at them
Not scared or angry
But wanting to play
These monsters of the trees
Fled before the fat pink baby

The joyful little nudist
Chased them all round the wood
Babbling nonsense
Not that English would have done any good
The snakes ducked into holes
The spiders climbed to aerial strongholds
They peered from shelter
At the bizarre, giggling creature

Tired finally from the chase
Bare ass baby plopped down
On the ground
A fountain of gold from his tiny wrinkled weenis
arced across the morning sky
An acrid rainbow to start the day
Then he shat all over the forest
Like the devil's own cannon, his anus
The fetid stench of baby poo
ruined the outside
A skunk awoke, held its nose, and ran away
And baby began to cry

The wails set the trunks to trembling
The birds to screeching
The wolves to howling
All the forest critters a clamoring
Even the river fish peaked into the surface
Just to discover the commotion

Old Bear woke from her slumber
Her alarm not yet set to awake her
A moment it took
To clear the eyes and the mind
And realize what was occurring
Then her mind wrapped itself around
The reality of the sound
The horrific, ear splitting, caterwaul
Disrupting her zen

With a growl and rumble
Old Bear tumbled from her nest
Loose skin rolling
Across remaining layers of fat
While the bristly brown fur
Knotted and matted
Shed in clumps
Blanketing the cavern floor

Lumbering into the open
Discovering all the forest aflutter
Warnings of danger
Rapidly transfered
Flowing and growing like a river
So Old Bear followed the sound
To its source
To discover
For herself
What was the problem
And why it had to be so damn loud

The next clearing over
The source of the discord, discovered
Approaching slowly
The tiny, pink bastard kept howling
She screamed in its face
To shut up and surrender
But the enemy cared not
Only screaming louder
So Old Bear drew deep its breath
and from the bottom of its belly

Let loose a roar
That would have impressed a storm
A whirlwind in his face
A tremor in his eardrums
And still the little nude squealer
Just kept on screaming

The forest folk grew restless and scared
This tiny beast seemed impossible to defeat
Then Old bear rose up on her hind legs
Swung her paw round her body
Tall and wide
Smashed it down upon the tiny howling beast
With a pop and squirt
its blood splattered
Its bones cracked
Its flesh tore like a paper sack
and silence fell
On the forest once more
and Old Bear
Returned home
A Hero of the Forest Folk
Having vanquished the terrorist
The foreigner
The barbarian in their midst.

JD Adler

Dividends

In the grass lay a pig
Covered in mud
Cool and thick
Warmed by the noon sun
On its fat, pink flesh

Across the yard, he spied
Thick curly piles of white
As the sheep were shorn
The farmer's daughters sat on stools
Running sheers and gossiping
A chorus of "baa's" echoing
Over the open yard

Pig smelled the mud
As he laid all alone
And grew to hate the sheep
For stealing his due

He gathered the hogs
Spoke to the poke in a fiery tone
Of the inequities they endured
At the duplicitous hooves
Of the sheep and the goats
Taking up all the space
Eating all the oats
Never used to be here
Now they acted like
This farm was theirs

The pigs they got to snorting
Angered at the suffering
They discovered they were enduring
When the sun went down
And the humans went indoors
A drove of the pink, mud splattered creatures
Charged across the yard
Ramming the sheep

Stomping their nests
Till the entire flock fled
And the farm belonged
to the pigs once again

A few months passed
The Drove of Pigs
Enjoyed their status
As the most valued animals
On the farm

Then the day came
Late October
A chill in the air
Leaves brown and gold
Fell to ground
And the farmer's daughters came
To herd the pigs into the far barn
Where they had never gone before

One by one
They were led into a room
Where the son stood with a blade
Each and every pig
Throat cut and body bled
Knew with pride
None of those damn sheep
Would be replacing them

JD Adler

The Sand Bar

One sunny morn'
Along the sea shore
Amidst the white sands
And red coral reefs
A Purple Octopus
And an Orange Platypus
Sat at a sand bar
debating faith vs logic
Against the backdrop
Of surviving long enough
to die

Along came a Swan
All silver and shiny
And settled softly
On the shore
He smiled and stated
everything mentioned
was garbage
From Plato to Thoreau, Pythagorus to Hawking
None of it was worth the ink
For he knew for some time now
That nothing was real
All that we see is imagined

Octopus raised a tentative tentacle
Inquiring quite curiously
How can we possibly perceive
through the eye of our mind
the very same sun in the very same sky
If we all only see what we believe?
Platypus he nodded his odd noggin knowingly
Clearly comforted by the logic

The silver swan's feathers
Ruffled and shimmered
As he laughed at the octo-pothesis.
"How do you know I see what you see

The Adler Collection

That to me, these rocks are not flowers,
And what you call flying
I don't see as
walking around
My feet firmly upon the ground?"

Platypus was perplexed
And quite concerned
There seemed no way to know
What if the world was not what it seemed
But something else entirely?

Octopus grew angry
Changing from purple to grey
Planting its tentacles
Raising its head
looking the swan dead in the eye
He declared definitively
"Your proposition is preposterous
Made up madness
There is only one truth
Which contains all of us
Anything else would be chaos
Which is clearly not what we see."

Swan looked at Platypus askew
Conspiracy plain in his beak
his tongue silver and smooth
He drew him under his wing
"We must stick together
Brothers of a bill
These cultists want us to surrender
Telling us to believe
what they have agreed
Just because they have books that say so
But if I am correct
And everything is always
As you perceive
Then everything is equally true

And no matter the method you use
You will always find what you seek."
The Platypus's brain
Could not explain
All these contradictions
"If my facts and your facts
Were equally accurate
Even though not the same
Then nothing was true
And all that I knew
was merely a fantasy
concocted in my own cranium."

The Platypus began to weep

Octopus scolded the Swan
For filling his fragile friend with fear
Then turned, wrapped him in an octo-hug
And reassured the odd, oblong creature
That we were all bound together
By a truth universal

He explained the people and the sea
everything you see
are all specs of light
floating in a sea of night
cooling embers
of the explosion from which all originates

Platypus found none of this comforting
And all of it confusing
He grew quite convinced
that purple bastard
Was trying to trick him
With all his clever word play

Then he remembered this all started
When that weird fucker came onto land
So he swung round real fast
with his big wide tail
and slapped that Octopus
Off the sand
into the waves
To be carried away
And never trouble him again

Then he began
To pile up rock and sand
Building a sea wall
To keep off the land
The tricky purple prick
Who wanted to deceive him
with his fancy explanations
Of an objective truth

And the Swan joined in
Flapping his wings
Billowing sand in the air
Together they worked
Towards common goal
To keep out the one
Who said
such a thing could be done.

JD Adler

Tragic Myth

In the muck of a rock
spinning in space
the gods
concocted
a creature
who could crawl from the seas
to paint the caves
with images from their dreams

and to kill

everything the creatures see
they eat, carve, or destroy,
They kill the world
The gods provided
And everything it held
Even killing themselves
 with their own entertainment
Kill, Kill, Kill
And what they don't kill
They fuck
Fuck, Fuck, Fuck
Till it can't be fucked no more
Then leave it behind
Like a finished meal

In between the killing and the fucking
They build a civilization
out of corpses and chemicals
That tear into the earth
And stab into the sky
And they shuttle about
In boxes that burn
the fossilized flesh
of those who came before
Befouling their own air and
Destroying generations yet to be born

The Adler Collection

Then this creation grew bolder still
Took to the skies
higher and higher they did rise
Penetrating the veil of night
till they were able to look
the gods
in the eyes

When they saw fear
In the faces
of their Creators
they laughed out loud
and fucked their gods
Right in the ass
Not a reach-around proffered
and when then they were done
Violating the divine bums
they killed
every last one
of those who gave them
Body and breath
And the imagination
To rise from the depths

now alone
in the 'verse
The creature turned and looked
for the next frontier to conquer
To destroy and remake
In their own polluted vision

But all the universe
Was barren and bleak
Emptied by lust and greed
they'd destroyed
their own sustenance
and so, in the end,
they'd fucked themselves

To death

JD Adler

www.ingramcontent.com/pod-product-compliance
Lightning Source LLC
Chambersburg PA
CBHW070439010526
44118CB00014B/2109